Summer Solstice

BY MADDIE SPALDING

The Child's World®
childsworld.com

Published by The Child's World®
1980 Lookout Drive • Mankato, MN 56003-1705
800-599-READ • www.childsworld.com

Photographs ©: iStockphoto, cover, 1, 4–5, 8–9, 13, 16–17, 19, 20–21; Shutterstock Images, 6–7, 14; Yan Lev/Shutterstock Images, 11–12; Red Line Editorial, 22

ISBN 9781503823822
LCCN 2017944899

Printed in the United States of America
PA02358

ABOUT THE AUTHOR
Maddie Spalding is a writer and editor who lives in Minnesota. She has written more than 20 books for children. Her favorite summertime activity is spending time with family at their lakeside cabin.

Contents

The Longest Day

Today is the summer solstice. It is the first day of summer!

It is the longest day of the year. The sun rises early in the morning.

It is the shortest
night of the year.
The sun sets late
at night.

9

Earth **tilts** toward the sun. Part of Earth gets more sunlight. This makes the summer **season**.

The Start of Summer

Earth has two halves.
The North Pole is in the
Northern **Hemisphere**.
The South Pole is in the
Southern Hemisphere.

North Pole

South Pole

Summer begins in June in the Northern Hemisphere. The North Pole tilts toward the sun.

Sunrise and Sunset

People celebrate
the summer solstice.
They watch the
sun rise.

It is a sunny day.

People walk to the park.

They have a **picnic**.

19

After today, the days get shorter. Soon it will be fall.

21

Paper Plate Sun Craft

Make your own paper sun!

Supplies:

1 paper plate
yellow and black paint
paint brush
orange construction paper
yellow construction paper
scissors

Instructions:

1. Paint the paper plate yellow. Let it dry.

2. Cut out five triangles from the orange construction paper. Then cut out five triangles from the yellow construction paper. Glue them around the paper plate on the side that is not painted.

3. Using the black paint, paint a face on your paper plate sun!

Glossary

hemisphere—(HEM-i-sfeer) A hemisphere is one half of a round object. Earth has a Northern hemisphere and a Southern hemisphere.

picnic—(PIK-nik) A picnic is a meal eaten outdoors. We have a picnic during the summer solstice.

season—(SEE-zuhn) A season is one of the four natural parts of the year. The summer solstice is the start of the summer season.

tilts—(TILTS) Something tilts when it leans to one side. Part of the Earth tilts toward the sun during the summer solstice.

To Learn More

Books

Terp, Gail. *What Is a Solstice?* Mankato, MN: The Child's World, 2017.

Yee, Wong Herbert. *Summer Days and Nights*. New York, NY: Henry Holt and Company, 2012.

Web Sites

Visit our Web site for links about the summer solstice:
childsworld.com/links

Note to Parents, Teachers, and Librarians: We routinely verify our Web links to make sure they are safe and active sites. So encourage your readers to check them out!

Index